Teen Alcoholism

Look for these and other books in the Lucent
Overview series:

Teen Alcoholism

by Nancy J. Nielsen

LUCENT
B·O·O·K·S

LUCENT Overview Series

Library of Congress Cataloging-in-Publication Data

Nielsen, Nancy J.
    Teen alcoholism / by Nancy Nielsen.
        p.   cm. — (Lucent overview series)
    Includes bibliographical references and index.
    Summary: Discusses alcohol use and abuse among American teenagers, and describes some of the measures used in treatment and prevention of alcoholism.
    ISBN 1-56006-121-9
    1. Alcoholism—United States—Juvenile literature.   2. Teenagers—United States—Alcohol use—Juvenile literature   3. Alcohol —Physiological effects.—Juvenile literature.   [1. Alcoholism.   2. Teenagers —Alcohol use.]   I. Title.   II. Series.
    HV5066.N54   1990
    362.29'2'0835—dc20   90-6196
                                                                            CIP
                                                                            AC

© Copyright 1990 by Lucent B[...]
P.O. Box 289011, San Diego, CA [...]

To all recovering teenage alcoholics

Contents

Introduction

THE WIDESPREAD abuse of alcohol and other drugs by teenagers is a relatively new problem for our society. It has developed in just the past twenty-five years, but it is already a major problem. Statistics show that over 80 percent of high school seniors have used alcohol in the past year.

A 1986 study by the U.S. Department of Justice showed that the United States has the highest level of teen chemical abuse in the industrialized world. What is worse, the study showed that young people are trying drugs and alcohol at an increasingly early age. On the average, the first time a young person uses alcohol or drugs is between the ages of twelve and sixteen.

These haunting statistics prove that alcoholism is not just an adult's disease. Teenagers and even children can become physically and psychologically dependent upon alcohol. In fact, researchers say teens and children can become more easily addicted to alcohol than adults.

One reason for this is that teens drink for the sole purpose of getting drunk. They do not drink because they have learned to enjoy alcoholic beverages. Teens do not say things like, "A nice glass of wine would go well with dinner," or "A beer would taste good with this pizza." For teens, alcohol is simply a means to an end: getting drunk. To get drunk, one

(opposite page) Scenes like this are becoming increasingly common in our society. What accounts for the growing problem of teen alcoholism?

9

must always drink to excess. Teen drinkers, therefore, are often excessive drinkers. And excessive drinking increases one's chances of becoming addicted.

Another reason teens can easily become addicted to alcohol is that they are more likely to lose control of their drinking than an adult. Why? Because teenagers are still growing and developing, psychologically as well as physically. They have not developed the wisdom and strength of will to enable them to overcome the urge to escape life's difficulties. Therefore, once they begin using alcohol, teens are more likely to be unable to stop.

Why are young people turning to drugs and alcohol in unprecedented numbers? The reasons are many and complex. Some people argue that teens are just imitating their parents and other adults they see abusing drugs and alcohol. Others note that many teens feel their futures are bleak. The threat of

Two teens participate in an International Youth Year (1985) assembly. The theme of the assembly is the awareness of teen problems and aspirations. By teaching teens positive coping mechanisms, the assembly hopes to discourage alcohol and drug abuse.

nuclear war and AIDS, the prospect of spending their lives trapped in an unsatisfying job and with unwanted responsibilities, has darkened the horizon for many young people. Often, then, for teenagers, alcohol becomes a way to avoid their uncertain futures; to numb the fear and the pain.

What can be done to solve the growing problem of teen alcoholism? Many experts believe prevention through education is the best tactic. Informing teens and children about the harmful effects of alcohol to their bodies and minds can help motivate them to avoid its use in the first place. From a more positive standpoint, instilling children with self-esteem, pride in achievement, and hope for the future can take them a long way towards avoiding drug and alcohol abuse.

Teen alcoholism is an issue that needs to be faced now, both by teens and adults. It will not go away by itself. Adults must work together with young people to discover the roots of this problem and develop creative solutions. A young person's future is too valuable to waste on the tragedy of alcoholism.

1

A History of Alcohol

BEER. WINE. LIQUOR. All have been around for centuries and have become ingrained in the customs of people all over the world. All three drinks are also intoxicating substances that can cause drunkenness. Understanding the history of alcohol, society's changing attitudes toward it, and the role it has played in various cultures may help shed some light on why drinking alcoholic beverages is so popular and why solving the problems it causes is such a complex issue.

Beer

The first intoxicating drink was probably some form of beer. The ancient Babylonians considered beer a gift from the gods. They brewed it in their religious temples as early as 5000 B.C.

Drinking beer was also widespread in ancient Egypt. Called *hek*, it was made from barley bread. First the bread was crumbled into jars. Then it was covered with water and allowed to ferment.

The Egyptian pharaohs blessed large quantities of this beer in honor of Isis, the goddess of nature. Then they distributed two jugs of beer daily to each peasant worker, free of charge. Not surprisingly,

(opposite page) With several kegs of beer on hand, members of the Liederkranz *club prepare to celebrate the end of Prohibition in 1933. Today, the use of alcoholic beverages is popular in the United States.*

13

drunkenness was a common problem in ancient Egypt.

Other countries around the world had their own kinds of beer. The natives of South and Central America, for example, fermented corn into a beer called *chicha*. Roots of pepper plants were fermented into an intoxicating drink called *kava* in the South Sea Islands. The Vikings and other Germanic

Today, beer is brewed in mass quantities. Beer making has its roots in the Babylonian culture, which brewed beer as early as 5000 B.C.

The king of the ancient Saxons passes the drinking horn at Christmas time. Beer was often included in religious ceremonies and celebrations.

tribes drank huge quantities of beer made from grain and a plant called hops. Africans made an alcoholic drink from fermented palm leaves.

Wine

Wine making is as ancient a practice as brewing beer. King Jamshid of Persia is usually credited with the discovery of wine, several thousand years before the time of Christ. Because he loved to eat grapes, King Jamshid ordered his servants to store extra grapes in a few large jars in the palace cellar. Several months later, he called for his grapes only to find that the skins had burst. All that remained in

Wine, shown here with the grapes used in its production, was discovered accidently by the Persian King Jamshid, who often stored grapes in his cellar.

The counterpart of Dionysus is Bacchus, the Roman god of wine and fertility. In 186 B.C., the senate banned drinking festivals held in his honor, believing that such celebrations were morally corrupt.

the jars was a dark purple juice. Disappointed, Jamshid instructed his servants to label the jars poison and return them to the cellar.

A short time later, one of the women of the court was intent on committing suicide. She found the jars labeled poison and drank some of the juice. To her surprise, the drink made her feel happy and relaxed.

She told the king about the pleasant effects of the dark juice. Jamshid tried the drink himself and was pleased. He declared that a share of grapes from every harvest should be preserved in the same manner.

Wine was also popular in both ancient Greece and the Roman Empire. A Greek myth attributes its widespread use to Dionysus, the Greek god of wine. His counterpart in Roman mythology is Bacchus. Great quantities of wine were drunk at festivals in honor of these gods.

Even though the Greeks and Romans added water to their wine to reduce its strength, people still became drunk. Nevertheless, excessive drinking and drunkenness were frowned upon. Because the Dionysian festivals, celebrations in honor of Dionysus that involved the drinking of wine, eventually turned into drunken orgies, the Roman senate banned them in 186 B.C.

Wine played an important role in the early Christian church, too, and is mentioned 165 times in the Bible. The Gospels report that Jesus drank wine and even turned water into wine at a wedding feast. Christians drank wine as a part of their religious services because to them it symbolized the blood of Christ. In fact, much of the knowledge of how to

The physiological effects of alcohol have been recorded throughout history. The caption of this early nineteenth-century French photograph reads: "Ah! I'm losing. I can hardly see and I'm getting fuddled. Alcohol dulls even the clearest mind."

A worker pumps wine from a barrel at a Napa Valley winery. Even without such modern wine-making equipment, people throughout the ages discovered ways to ferment grapes and other fruits.

grow grapes and make wine has been handed on by Christian monks throughout the centuries.

Besides being part of religious ceremonies, wine was often drunk in preference to water because it was safer. Alexander the Great, during his campaigns to conquer the world, often camped with his army near swamps and drank wine mixed with water because the water alone was too polluted. And in London during the nineteenth century, people did not drink the water because they rightly suspected it of spreading disease. Even the poorest people often drank wine instead.

Liquor

Stronger alcoholic drinks, called liquor or spirits, were discovered by an Arabian alchemist named Geber in the eighth century A.D. He burned away the impurities that form in wine during fermentation and isolated the remaining liquid. This chemical process is called distillation. The result was a more

Stronger alcoholic drinks are created through distillation. This Scotch whiskey, for example, is distilled from malted barley.

concentrated liquid with a higher alcoholic content.

Liquor was not discovered in Europe, however, until five hundred years later. Arnaud de Villeneuve, a French professor of medicine, made a concentrated liquid from wine called brandywine, later shortened to brandy. De Villeneuve claimed that brandy was a single cure for all of humanity's diseases. It "prolongs life, clears away ill humors, revives the heart and maintains youth," he said.

In the 1600s, another professor of medicine, this time in Holland, experimented with distilling the fermented barley used for making beer, and produced gin. A similar drink called vodka was produced in Russia. Then the Scandinavians distilled a liquid made from fermented potatoes and called it akvavit. The Irish discovered that whiskey could be made from malted barley by adding yeast to make it ferment.

In early America, whiskey was made from rye, a local grain. The Americans also invented bourbon, a distilled alcoholic drink made from corn, in the 1700s.

Problems with drunkenness

Because physicians in the sixteenth century told the European people that drinking was good for their health, liquor came to be widely consumed in Europe. But along with the use of spirits came the problems of drinking too much and drunkenness.

At this time most Europeans took their physicians' advice and drank alcohol to improve their health. They thought they could not live without alcohol, and believed a daily glass of it was needed to clear the head and keep the heart in good working order. No field laborer was expected to do a hard day's work without the aid of a stiff drink.

At first, drinking alcohol was a family affair. Families shared a glass of beer or wine at the dinner table. Even very young children were given alcohol

This 1846 lithograph, titled The Progress of Intemperance: An Invitation to Drink *illustrates the prevalence of drunkenness in Britain during the nineteenth century.*

to drink. Eventually, however, men began to drink outside their homes, gathering at local taverns for drinks after a day's work. This practice increased the amount of drunkenness among men.

It became a common practice for Englishmen to boast about being drunk and about their abilities to drink great quantities of beer or whiskey. Laws and punishments against drunkenness did little to curtail the problem.

Drunkenness became so widespread in Great Britain in the sixteenth and seventeenth centuries that the country was referred to as a nation of drunkards. Many paintings and wood carvings depict the great social problems that overdrinking caused in England during this time, such as unemployment and wife and child abuse.

The Pilgrims brought beer to America in 1620. Even their choice of Plymouth Rock as a place to land was influenced by their supply of beer. "For we could not take much time for further search and consideration, our victuals being much spent, especially beer," wrote their leader, William Bradford.

Colonists who arrived later added whiskey to their cargo of alcoholic beverages. However, the leaders of the colonies frowned upon drunkenness. Those who became intoxicated by alcohol were often punished and ridiculed for having little self-control.

After the American revolutionary war in which the colonists won their freedom from Great Britain, drinking increased. Without England's economic controls, beer and whiskey became cheaper. More people could afford to buy them, and to buy more of them.

Soon alcoholism, or addiction to alcohol, became

The pioneering American physician Benjamin Rush was one of the first to suggest that alcohol was unhealthy. In 1784, he published articles outlining the health hazards associated with alcohol.

a widespread problem in the United States of America. In the late 1700s, President Thomas Jefferson claimed that "one-third of the people in the United States are killing themselves with whiskey."

One of the first people in the United States to suggest that alcohol was unhealthy was Dr. Benjamin Rush, an American physician. In 1784 he wrote that the use of spirits could cause liver problems, jaundice, hoarseness, diabetes, epilepsy, gout, madness, and frequent belching.

Temperance

The first temperance societies, which supported abstinence from drinking, were formed in the United States as a result of Dr. Rush's writings. Members pledged to use no wine or liquors "except by the advice of a physician, or in case of actual disease." At the end of the first year, temperance society members held a meeting. Many were surprised to find

An 1859 portrait of the family of Lyman Beecher, the clergyman from Connecticut who started an antidrinking crusade in 1810.

that avoiding spirits had not caused their health to suffer. And many members reported they were able to work more efficiently when not drinking alcohol.

Soon many preachers were speaking against the use of alcohol. One of the most outspoken was Reverend Lyman Beecher who started an antidrinking crusade in 1810. His sermons were full of messages to save the country from "rum-selling, tippling folk, infidels, and ruff-scruff."

Gradually, attitudes toward drinking began to change. Employers, who once thought alcohol was needed to sustain their workers, stopped serving it to them. Liquor rations were discontinued in the United States Army. More and more people joined the American Temperance Union, pledging total abstinence from the drinking of alcoholic beverages.

The question of whether or not to drink alcohol developed into a major national conflict. Many peo-

This lithograph titled Principles of the Prohibition Party *appeared in 1888. Despite such efforts to depict the evils of alcohol, drunkenness and alcohol consumption continued.*

During Prohibition, federal agents discover a hidden cache of illegal alcohol. Prohibition, which went into effect in 1920, was unpopular and difficult to enforce.

ple who had seen the ill effects of drunkenness in their towns and within their families worked hard to rid the country of alcohol altogether. Many states passed laws against the sale of alcohol.

For years people continued to lobby and work against the use of alcohol in the United States. One of the strongest groups favoring prohibition was the Anti-Saloon League. It began working for the passage of an amendment to the U.S. Constitution that would prohibit the sale of alcohol.

Despite the efforts of the temperance workers, the use of alcohol increased in the early 1800s. Many people still believed they could not live without it. Groups that supported the drinking of alcohol worked hard to stop the prohibitionists.

Gradually, the temperance movement gained strength. Finally, in 1919, the Eighteenth Amendment to the Constitution was passed by both the House and the Senate, and was quickly ratified by thirty-six states. The amendment prohibited the manufacture, importation, exportation, transportation, and sale of alcoholic beverages in the United States.

Prohibition

Prohibition went into effect in 1920. But it was an unpopular law and many Americans refused to obey it. Soon law-enforcement officials found that the law was impossible to enforce.

Because the amendment did not prohibit the possession of alcohol, many people stocked up before the law went into effect. Also, liquor was manufactured in other countries and smuggled into the United States. Bootleggers, illegal manufacturers in

A model of a moonshiner's vat attracts visitors to the Catoctin Mountains National Park in Maryland. Each weekend, park officials produce an undrinkable moonshine for demonstration purposes only.

Al Capone, Prohibition era gang leader, participated in the St. Valentine's Day Massacre.

the United States, made and sold it to interested consumers. Much of what they made, however, was impure and unfit to drink. People became sick and some even died from drinking bootleg alcohol.

It seemed that the amendment whose purpose was to stop the drinking of alcoholic beverages was having the opposite effect. Many people started to make alcohol at home. Others visited speakeasies, places where alcoholic beverages were sold illegally, and attended parties where gin was made in bathtubs. So many people were breaking the law that it was impossible to stop them. Another effect was that drinking alcohol became common among new groups. Before Prohibition, most American consumers of alcohol were men. Now, unexpectedly, women and young people started to see drinking as a smart or popular thing to do.

The government hired prohibitionist agents to restore law and order. But many of the agents were dishonest or even bootleggers themselves. Violent clashes broke out in the streets. So many lawbreakers were arrested that the prison populations almost doubled in three years. The courts had more cases than they could handle.

Gangsters such as Al Capone were making big profits from bootlegging. At first, people were fascinated by the colorful lives of the gangsters. Caught up in the excitement of the era, Americans supported, or at least failed to discourage, the behavior of these criminals.

Then, an event in 1929 changed the way people viewed the gangsters. On February 14, a group of bootleggers in Chicago murdered an opposing group of bootleggers. This cold and brutal killing came to be known as the St. Valentine's Day Massacre. It was soon followed by other gangster-related events of violence.

The fighting and unrest caused by the Eighteenth Amendment scared the public. Many who had wanted Prohibition now began to speak out against

Under Franklin D. Roosevelt, Prohibition was repealed with the passing of the Twenty-first Amendment in 1933.

With the demise of Prohibition, the alcohol industry boomed in many states. Here, malt whiskey is distilled in onion-shaped pot stills.

it. They hoped repealing the law would stop the violence.

Franklin D. Roosevelt promised voters that the Eighteenth Amendment was doomed should he be elected president. He was, and in 1933, Prohibition was repealed with the passing of the Twenty-first Amendment to the United States Constitution.

Today's attitudes toward alcohol

The use of alcoholic beverages is still popular in the United States today. The average American adult drinks two and three-quarters gallons of alcohol per year. And most teenagers have tried beer, wine, or liquor before they graduate from high school.

Alcoholism is a major problem in the United States. More than ten million adults are alcoholics, while another eight million are heavy drinkers. Alcoholism is the number one drug-abuse problem among American youth.

Fortunately, society has developed new ways of dealing with alcoholism. Most schools offer drug and alcohol education. Teenagers are becoming aware of the problems of alcoholism and are making decisions about the use of alcohol that will prevent them from becoming alcoholics in the future.

2

The Physical Effects of Alcohol

ALCOHOL IS THE intoxicating part of beer, wine, and liquors—the part that causes drunkenness. It is formed during fermentation, the process that creates the alcoholic beverage. When sugars from the fruits or grains are combined with yeast and water, alcohol results.

Alcohol is a drug and, like all drugs, it has an effect on a person's body and mind. Because drinking alcoholic beverages makes some people feel more alive and become more outgoing, alcohol is sometimes seen as a stimulant. But in fact it is a depressant, and slows down the central nervous system, of which the brain is a part. Small amounts of alcohol can affect a person's coordination and judgment. Drinking a large amount of alcohol at one time can even cause death.

Alcohol contributes to disease

Alcohol is also poisonous. It must be broken down and removed from the body. However, it leaves behind toxins, or poisons, that can cause health problems and contribute to serious diseases.

Beer contains the least amount of alcohol, about 3 to 6 percent. Wine is 8 to 14 percent alcohol. Ex-

(opposite page) Alcohol drinkers frequently lose inhibitions, coordination, and judgment. This nineteenth-century lithograph depicts a gentleman in an alcohol-induced state of reverie.

31

Because of its high alcoholic content, liquor is often diluted with fruit juices, soda, tonic, or other liquids.

tra alcohol is added to some wines such as sherry and port. These wines, called fortified wines, contain 18 to 21 percent alcohol.

Distilled spirits have a much higher alcoholic content. The alcoholic content of gin, scotch, vodka, whiskey, rum, and bourbon is about 40 percent. The amount of alcohol in liquor is measured as proof. One proof means 0.5 percent alcohol. A drink that contains 40 percent alcohol is called 80 proof. A bottle of 100 proof whiskey is 50 percent, or half, alcohol. Because their alcoholic content is so high, spirits are usually mixed in a drink with tonic, water, soda, or fruit juice.

Brandy, cognac, and cordials are also distilled spirits, sometimes called liqueurs. These sweet drinks contain between 20 and 65 percent alcohol. They are often served at the end of a meal and in small quantities for slow sipping.

Some people think they cannot get drunk from beer or wine because the alcoholic content is so low. That is not true. There is about as much alcohol in a twelve-ounce can of beer or in a five-ounce glass of wine as in a one-ounce shot of 80 proof liquor. A person must drink more beer or wine than liquor in order to get drunk, but intoxication is still possible.

The alcohol in alcoholic beverages, called ethyl alcohol or ethanol, should not be confused with other kinds of alcohol. Wood alcohol is sometimes used in fuels or paint products. Rubbing alcohol can be found in most homes as a medicine for aching muscles or for cleaning infected skin. Both wood and rubbing alcohol are very poisonous if swallowed.

What happens to alcohol in the body?

Within minutes of entering the stomach, as much as 20 percent of the alcohol in a drink is absorbed into the bloodstream. The rest remains in the stomach where it stimulates the secretion of gastric juices. These juices normally aid in the digestion of food. Large amounts of alcohol entering an empty stomach can irritate the gastric lining and cause the stomach to become inflamed.

From the stomach, the alcohol passes into the small intestine. Here the rest of it is absorbed through the intestinal wall and into the bloodstream. From the bloodstream, about 5 percent of alcohol leaves the body unchanged through urine, sweat, or exhaled breath.

Next the alcohol travels via the bloodstream to the heart. Small amounts of alcohol produce a slight increase in heart rate and blood pressure. Larger amounts reduce the pumping power of the heart and can cause an irregular heartbeat. The heart then pumps the alcohol through the blood vessels to other parts of the body, including the brain.

The brain is made up of millions of nerve cells

called neurons that send and receive messages to and from various parts of the body through the central nervous system. (The brain sends messages via the neurons that tell muscles to move, for example. Hunger and pain are examples of messages received by the brain.) Even small amounts of alcohol cause the neurons to fire less vigorously. Larger amounts can make them stop completely, disrupting messages to and from the brain.

Because the brain controls the central nervous system, any impairment of the brain affects many body functions, including vision, hearing, speech, and movements. It is this impairment that people refer to as being intoxicated or drunk.

Alcohol is also pumped from the heart to the liver

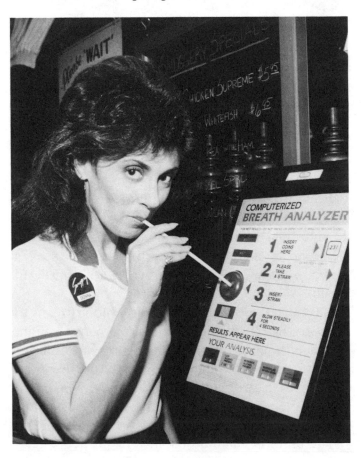

A woman tests an electronic breath analyzer, which analyzes components in the breath to determine blood alcohol level. It gives both a visual and verbal readout.

via the bloodstream. The liver is the only organ that can metabolize, or break down, alcohol so it can be removed from the body. The liver removes alcohol from the blood through a process called oxidation, which changes alcohol into water, carbon dioxide, and energy. The liver can oxidize about one ounce of alcohol an hour. If a person drinks more than that, the alcohol must wait in the bloodstream until the liver can oxidize it. The more a person drinks, the more alcohol becomes stored in the blood.

Blood alcohol concentration

Legally, intoxication is measured by the amount of alcohol in the bloodstream. The buildup of alcohol in the bloodstream is called the blood alcohol concentration (BAC). People with more than 0.05 percent alcohol in their blood are considered to be impaired by it. This means that there is 1 part alcohol for every 2,000 parts blood—one-twentieth of 1 percent.

Alcohol consumption impairs the nervous system, affecting one's ability to drive safely. Here, an alcohol-related accident seems to mock an anti-drinking storefront display.

John Bonham (top) of the rock group Led Zeppelin died in 1980 after a bout of heavy drinking. After drinking the equivalent of forty shots of vodka, Bonham's liver was unable to process the alcohol in his system, resulting in toxic poisoning.

At a BAC of about 0.05 percent, thoughts and judgments become impaired and ordinary anxieties and inhibitions are relaxed. Many people find this to be a pleasurable experience. Often they feel freer, less shy, and more talkative.

As the BAC increases, the depressant effects of alcohol become more apparent. At 0.10 percent, voluntary motor actions, or movements, become clumsy. It takes longer to react to visual or auditory stimuli, a great danger for anyone driving a car. It is against the law in most states for people to drive if their blood alcohol concentration is 0.10 or higher.

At 0.20 percent, the entire motor area of the brain becomes depressed, or stops working, and a person may stagger. The part of the brain that controls emotional behavior also becomes depressed, causing underlying emotions to surface. That is why some people become happy under the influence of alcohol, while others become sad. Others become rowdy and even violent.

At 0.30 percent BAC, drinkers become very confused. They may become stuporous or pass out. Or, they may experience a blackout in which they say and do things they cannot later remember.

At 0.40 percent, the person becomes comatose or unconscious, and can die. This is called acute alco-

An Indiana trooper displays the Alco-Sensor II, a portable device that will allow on-site testing of suspected drunk drivers.

holic poisoning. The brain center, which controls respiration, becomes so depressed by alcohol that the person stops breathing.

About one thousand people in the United States die from alcohol overdoses each year. A sixteen-year-old Boston boy died recently when he drank a pint of vodka nonstop. His liver was not able to process enough of the alcohol in time to bring down his blood alcohol level. John Bonham of the rock group Led Zeppelin also died in 1980 after drinking the equivalent of forty shots of vodka.

Others die from choking on their vomit after a drinking bout. Heavy drinking often causes vomiting, either by direct irritation of the gastric lining of the stomach or as a protective response of the nervous system to an overdose of toxins. Wills Kelly, backup drummer for the rock group Meatloaf, died this way in London in 1984 after heavy drinking.

Intoxication

There is no set amount of alcohol a person must drink to reach a certain BAC level. The point at which intoxication is reached depends, among other things, on how fast the alcohol is consumed. For example, a person who drinks beverages containing four ounces of alcohol all at once may get drunk. That same person drinking the same amount over a period of four hours may not.

It also depends on whether a person is drinking on an empty stomach. It takes alcohol more time to be absorbed into the bloodstream when the stomach is full than when it is empty.

The size of the person also affects the percentage of alcohol in the bloodstream. A large person can drink more alcohol than a small person before becoming drunk. A person who weighs 160 pounds would reach a BAC of 0.05 by having two drinks in an hour. In contrast, a person who weighs 120 pounds could reach a BAC of 0.05 from one drink,

College students playing on a beach during Spring break. By channeling their energy into healthy activities, young people may avoid becoming entrenched in alcoholism.

and could be too intoxicated to drive after two drinks.

Those who drink more alcohol than their bodies can handle may wake up the next morning with a hangover. Although they are no longer drunk, they feel sick. They may have a headache from the toxins the alcohol left behind. They feel nauseous and may vomit from the alcohol's irritation of the stomach's lining. Because alcohol dehydrates the body, it may cause a person to be thirsty. Another symptom of a hangover is tiredness or fatigue.

Many people think they can speed up the oxidation process by drinking coffee, taking a cold shower, or exercising. But there is nothing a person can do to make the liver process alcohol more quickly. The only cure for a hangover is time.

Frequent excessive drinking can lead to alcoholism—a physical dependence on, or addiction to, alcohol. Such persons suffer from withdrawal symptoms when they stop drinking. Their bodies may start to shake, and they could go into convulsions. They also sweat, panic, and have trouble sleeping. Their pulse quickens and they may have a fever. They may even hallucinate, or imagine things that are not really happening.

The most serious form of alcohol withdrawal is called delirium tremens (d.t.'s). Instead of the withdrawal symptoms clearing in two or three days, they get worse. In addition to increased shakiness and profuse sweating, persons suffering from d.t.'s undergo periods of intense confusion and anxiety. Hallucinations become stronger and more terrifying; the person may "see" bugs on the walls and "feel" insects crawling all over the body. In this heightened state of agitation and physical exhaustion, other medical complications such as a heart attack or respiratory failure may result. Despite good medical care, as many as 20 percent of persons who go into d.t.'s die.

Alcohol and disease

Continued use of alcohol also contributes to many serious diseases. A common problem caused by alcohol is liver disease. The liver can process just so much alcohol before becoming damaged. Then diseases such as hepatitis (inflamed liver) or a fatty liver result.

Cancer is another disease often associated with alcohol. Along with smoking, excessive drinking is one of the established risk factors for cancer listed by the National Cancer Institute. Some alcoholic beverages contain urethane, a known cancer-causing agent. Besides liver cancer, overdrinking can cause cancer of the mouth and the esophagus.

Abuse of alcohol can also increase blood pressure, and high blood pressure can lead to heart attacks and strokes. Also, heavy use of alcohol can

damage the heart's muscles.

Heavy abuse of alcohol can lead to permanent damage of the brain and nervous system. Anyone who drinks enough to become unconscious develops tiny brain hemorrhages. These cause brain cells to die because they are not receiving enough oxygen. The disruption of the communication between the brain and the nervous system may result in muscle and nerve damage throughout the body.

Another common brain disorder caused by excessive drinking is Wernicke-Korsakoff syndrome. The result of a nutritional deficiency to the brain, this syndrome is characterized by paralysis of eye movements and can lead to severe confusion and dementia, or insanity. If caught early enough, it can be treated with doses of thiamine and glucose.

Women who drink when they are pregnant can

An 1898 woodcut illustrates the crowded condition of a New York mental hospital. In the ninteenth century, alcoholism was often treated as a form of insanity. For example, people with Wernicke-Korsakoff syndrome—characterized by confusion, dementia or insanity—were often imprisoned in an establishment such as this.

harm their babies. When a pregnant woman of any age drinks alcohol, so does her baby. Her blood passes the alcohol to the fetus in the womb through the umbilical cord.

But a fetus is not prepared to deal with alcohol. Its liver cannot yet process the alcohol properly. As a result, the fetus is damaged. This is called fetal alcohol syndrome.

These babies are born alcoholics. They may already have liver disease and must go through withdrawal.

Babies whose mothers are heavy drinkers are often underweight. They may have birth defects, brain damage, or learning disabilities. Fetal alcohol syndrome is the third most common cause of mental retardation.

In addition, an alcoholic mother will have trouble nursing her baby because alcohol reduces her supply of milk. Also, she can pass the alcohol to her baby through her milk.

Even small amounts of drinking can harm a fetus or a newborn baby. For this reason, doctors tell pregnant women and nursing mothers not to drink at all.

Alcohol and health

Drinking even small amounts of alcohol can have other, less serious effects on one's health. For example, drinking can cause weight problems.

Many people do not realize how many calories are in alcoholic beverages. A twelve-ounce can of beer or four ounces of wine, for example, contain from 80 to 180 calories. An ounce of liquor has 65 to 85 calories. When mixed with soda or juices, a drink may contain as many as 300 calories!

Although alcoholic beverages contain calories, they are not good sources of nutrition. That is because most of the vitamins, minerals, or proteins in the fruits, grains, and yeast used to make them are

lost during processing. This is especially true during the distillation of spirits.

Many persons who drink large amounts of alcohol do not eat balanced meals. A lack of good nutrition shows up in their bodies in unhealthy ways. They may become weak, depressed, or have trouble sleeping.

Lack of good nutrition also affects one's appearance. A normal body keeps busy all day repairing its cells. But it must stop this work to process alcohol. When this happens too often, the body cannot keep up its everyday repairs. Problems such as broken blood vessels on the face, premature wrinkles, and puffiness around the eyes may result. Too much alcohol can also cause hair to lose its natural shine, or

Alcohol can harm a fetus or newborn baby. Here, a counselor tells pregnant teenagers about the deleterious effects of alcohol consumption during pregnancy.

even to fall out. Too much alcohol can make acne get worse.

Here is what the actress Brooke Shields says about the effects that drinking had on her appearance: "Alcohol disturbed my sleep and in turn diminished the clarity of my eyes the day after. . . . Even moderate drinking affects the skin and dehydrates the body. . . ." Alcohol and the resulting lack of good nutrition can also suppress the immune system. The immune system is a complex network including the thymus, lymph nodes, and white blood cells that work together to fight infections and allergens, or foreign substances such as pollen, that get in the bloodstream. This means that heavy drinkers

Three men gather on the street to share a drink. Because of the physiological and psychological risks associated with alcohol, some alcoholics lose jobs, homes, and family ties.

are more likely to get sick than others. The two million Americans who have allergies may find that alcohol's effect on their immune system makes their allergies worse.

In addition, many people are allergic to the grains and additives in alcohol. Those allergic to corn or wheat, for example, may forget that these grains are used in making beer and liquors. Other allergens found in alcoholic beverages include egg white, yeast, saccharin, sulfites, and food coloring.

Before deciding whether or not to use alcohol, teenagers need to consider the effects alcohol has on the body and the health risks associated with drinking—from acne to liver disease to cancer. When teens consider these factors, plus the widespread problem of teen alcoholism, many decide that the risks of drinking are not worth it.

Because alcohol use can affect one's physical appearance, former teen model and actress Brooke Shields advocates an alcohol-free lifestyle.

3

The Problem of Teen Alcoholism

TEEN ALCOHOLISM has become a big problem in the United States. About 3.3 million teenagers are problem drinkers. One-fourth of all seventh through twelfth graders admit to drinking at least once a week. In a survey, about 40 percent of twelfth graders reported having one episode of heavy drinking in the past two weeks.

Among New York public school seventh through twelfth graders, 11 percent described themselves as hooked on alcohol. The problem is widespread and involves teens from all over the country and from every social class.

Statistics on teen drinking

Since Prohibition, the number of teenagers who drink has risen steadily. In 1948, only 35 percent of high school students drank alcohol. In 1988, about 92 percent used it, according to a University of Michigan survey.

Heavy use of alcohol among high school seniors, however, has dropped slightly. In 1979, 7 percent of high school seniors reported drinking alcohol daily, according to the same survey. In 1988, only 5 percent, or one senior in twenty, reported drinking daily.

Various studies show that the amount of alcohol

(opposite page) A teenager stumbles across the street after a drinking bout.

47

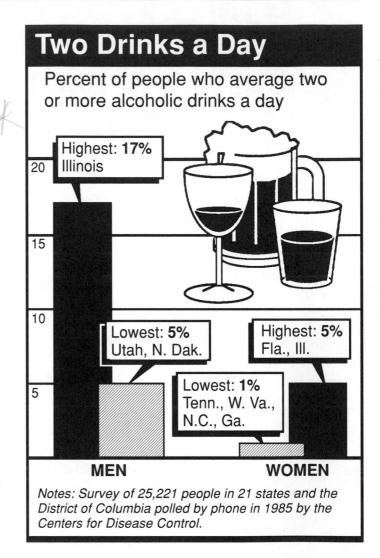

Two Drinks a Day

Percent of people who average two or more alcoholic drinks a day

Highest: **17%**
Illinois

20

15

10

Lowest: **5%**
Utah, N. Dak.

Highest: **5%**
Fla., Ill.

Lowest: **1%**
Tenn., W. Va.,
N.C., Ga.

5

MEN

WOMEN

Notes: Survey of 25,221 people in 21 states and the District of Columbia polled by phone in 1985 by the Centers for Disease Control.

consumed by teenagers differs according to geographical location. More teens in the northeastern and north-central parts of the United States indicate that they drink more than do teens in other parts of the country. Also, teens who live in the suburbs use alcohol more than teens who live in cities.

Statistics also seem to indicate that family situations influence teen drinking patterns. Teens who come from one-parent homes or from families with problems are more likely to drink. And boys who say their parents approve of their drinking are twice as likely to say that they are heavy drinkers as boys whose parents disapprove of drinking.

Researchers have also found that the age at which children take their first drink is decreasing. In 1988, the first drink was usually taken around age twelve, compared to age thirteen to fourteen in the 1940s and 1950s. According to a *Weekly Reader* survey, more than 33 percent of fourth graders say children their age push each other to try beer, wine or liquor.

Patterns of drinking differ between boys and girls, the research shows. Boys drink more than girls, but girls are catching up. In 1975, 42 percent of girls first used alcohol before the tenth grade. Since 1981, 52 percent of girls have used it before the tenth grade. Nearly one-half of boys and more than one-fourth of girls among high school seniors in 1985 reported heavy drinking (five or more drinks in a row) on at least one occasion two weeks before answering a National Council on Alcoholism survey.

Studies indicate that teens who come from a one-parent home are more likely to drink. This single mother spends quality time with her son to make up for the absence of a father figure.

Although many factors, such as age, gender, and location, seem to influence whether a teen drinks, statistics indicate that economic factors have little effect on alcohol use among teens. Alcohol may be more available in affluent families (statistics show that 95 percent of them have open bars in their homes), but teens from such families do not drink any more than teens from lower- and middle-class families.

Teens tend to drink more than adults on occasions when they do drink, according to the studies. This is of special concern to chemical-dependency counselors. Teenagers get drunk more easily because they are smaller and less experienced drinkers than adults.

Such statistical information is helpful to community leaders as they plan alcohol-abuse prevention

Many people, such as this fan at a Red Sox game, tend to drink more alcohol during social events.

A street scene in New York City. Experts maintain that youths must be actively engaged in their community to avoid truancy and vagrancy.

programs. It reveals many facts such as who drinks, how much they drink, when they drink, where they drink, and factors that influence why they drink. However, statistics do little to explain why so many teenagers are turning to alcohol.

One teenage alcoholic

Mark J. is a teen alcoholic. He is the son of an alcoholic father and has four brothers and sisters who are alcoholics, too.

Mark remembers first tasting beer at age six when he would bring it to his father. "I'd open them and take a sip. I never got drunk," he says, "but knew even then that I liked the taste a lot."

When Mark was ten, he slept over at the home of a friend whose mother was gone for the night. "We mixed her whiskey with 7-Up," he recalls, "and got really drunk."

By the seventh grade, Mark was drinking beer every weekend and often on school nights. He also mixed alcohol with other drugs such as marijuana.

Youths participate in a group talk at a residential center for troubled teens. The resident in the center sports the sign, "I am a Sneak. Please help me," because he violated house rules.

Often he would stay home from school and drink beer while his mother was at work.

Finally, Mark's mother became suspicious. When Mark was fourteen, she put him in treatment for alcoholism. He stayed straight for a while, but soon he was drinking alcohol and smoking marijuana again with a cousin.

Mark had repeated problems with skipping school in order to drink. In the tenth grade, he was often drunk in class or suspended for truancy. In the eleventh grade, he quit high school.

Soon Mark began getting in trouble with the law. He was arrested three times in three weeks for driving while intoxicated and sent to jail. Then the court ordered Mark to enter treatment again for alcoholism. He was eighteen years old.

Mark's story is similar to that of many other teen alcoholics. It is not unusual for them to go through treatment and then back to alcohol. Use of alcohol often leads to problems with the law, and the teen is sent by the courts for further treatment.

Why do teenagers drink? ⁂

Despite community programs that make teens aware of the problems of alcoholism, teens continue to drink in large numbers. One reason is peer pressure, or going along with the crowd in order to get approval from one's friends.

"Young people use chemicals because everybody else is doing it," says Jim Heaslip, a chemical dependency counselor and coauthor of the book, *Young People and Drugs*. According to Heaslip, young people have trouble saying no when they are offered an alcoholic drink.

Peer pressure usually becomes a major influence on children after fifth grade. During this time, friends play a key role in influencing children's attitudes. Friendship and belonging to a group are especially important, and students want to be like their friends. In some ways, the approval of friends be-

Some experts believe that teens mimic parents who drink.

comes more important to these children than the approval of their families. They think that by drinking, they will be accepted by their friends and classmates who drink. About 90 percent of kids who get into serious trouble involving alcohol, such as theft or drunken driving, say they did it to please or impress their friends.

Another reason teenagers drink is because they are exposed to negative parental role models in the home. The parents drink and set an example for the children. Such children are sometimes given alcohol by their parents when they are still very young. Perhaps their parents think it is funny or cute to see the child drinking. Or perhaps they simply do not know any better.

Eleanor Harris was given alcoholic drinks at home at an early age. She comes from an affluent family in which her father is an alcoholic. Eleanor began drinking heavily as a teenager, following her

An 1840 painting titled The Drunkard's Children *depicts the unhealthy environment that nineteenth-century children of alcoholics endured.*

A young motorist fails a field sobriety test given by the Traffic Safety Awareness Task Force, an operation formed in 1982 to crack down on drunk drivers.

father's example. But it was not until her brother was admitted to an alcohol treatment program that Eleanor realized she also was an alcoholic. In her family, heavy drinking had become the norm.

Eleanor Harris eventually wrote a magazine article about her family and their problems with alcohol. She believes that young people who come from alcoholic families need to know that their risk of becoming alcoholics is much greater than for others. Those who are aware of their risk are much less likely to abuse alcohol, she says.

Why do some teens become alcoholics?

As with Mark and Eleanor, problems with alcoholism seem to run in families. Statistics show that seven million children below the age of eighteen live in alcoholic homes. Between one-fourth and one-third will become alcoholics themselves.

Researchers disagree as to why this problem tends to run in families. Some researchers think that

Experts disagree about the role of genetics in the development of alcoholism. However, studies of identical twins indicate that if one twin is an alcoholic, chances are great that the other twin will become an alcoholic.

the family environment plays a dominant role in teen alcoholism. Just as children learn to drink alcohol by following their parents' example, they will also drink heavily if that is what they see their parents doing.

Homes in which one or both parents are alcoholics do not provide a healthy environment for children to develop emotionally. Therapists who work with the children of alcoholics have found that children from such homes lack social skills and tend to be isolated and withdrawn. And alcohol is involved in 65 percent of child abuse cases. Many children from these homes drink to escape from the discomfort or pain of their family situations.

The Children of Alcoholics Foundation has formally stated that alcoholism is caused by child neglect. This occurs because alcoholic parents are not able to give their children "quality love," the Foundation says. Instead, such parents experience life through an alcoholic stupor that makes them unaware of their children's needs and problems. These families are known as dysfunctional.

Heaslip, however, says that no one really knows for sure why some teenagers become alcoholics.

Based on his work with teen alcoholics, he does not think that they have any more problems or more family dysfunction than teens in general.

Some researchers think that heredity plays a role in alcoholism. Their studies indicate that inherited genes may make certain people more likely to become alcoholics. These genes are passed from parents to children.

One recent genetic study examines the THIQ factor. THIQ stands for tetrahydroisoquinoline, the most addictive substance known to humans. Researchers believe that THIQ is produced in the brain when alcohol is introduced to someone whose brain is predisposed to making it. The presence of THIQ in the brain triggers a need for alcohol in addictive doses. The person drinks, and the alcohol produces more THIQ, causing the need for more alcohol.

Is alcoholism inherited?

Statistical studies about alcoholic families seem to point to a genetic, or inherited, cause of alcoholism, too. One study of identical twins, for example, revealed that if one twin is an alcoholic, there is a greater chance than average that the other twin also will be an alcoholic.

In another study, a doctor from the University of Kansas studied children who had been separated from their parents at birth. He found that the natural children of alcoholic parents were four times more likely to become alcoholics, even though they were not living with the biological parent.

A third study showed that the effects of overdrinking may be similar for individuals within a family. It was found that male alcoholics whose fathers were also alcoholics tended to suffer the same consequences of heavy drinking, such as blackouts or violent outbursts.

Perhaps both genetics and family environment play some role in a teenager's development of alco-

A suspected drunk driver hangs his head while awaiting a test to determine blood alcohol content. He is sitting in the Van for Intoxicated Drivers that roams the streets of Baton Rouge, Louisiana, searching for possible drunk drivers.

holism. Regardless of family background, each teen must take responsibility for his or her own problem before it can be overcome, according to Heaslip and other chemical-dependency counselors.

Problems caused by teen alcoholism

Teenagers rarely recognize when they have a problem with alcoholism. Eventually, however, their grades suffer and/or they have problems with truancy, stealing, and/or driving while drunk. These problems usually bring them to the attention of a parent, teacher, or other community leader. In this way, says Heaslip, teen alcoholics are identified by their behavior.

Teens who drink often develop problems with family members. About two million twelfth graders each year report getting in trouble with their parents because of drinking. Teen alcoholics may suddenly become untalkative and even hostile to parents and other family members. They may lie about their activities and steal in order to get money to pay for alcohol.

Teen alcohol abuse not only causes personal, school, and family problems; it also causes problems for society in general. Studies show that alcohol is a major contributing factor among teens involved in crime, suicide, pregnancy, auto accidents, and hospital admissions. About 40 percent of teen suicides and 30-60 percent of all assaults, rapes, and murders by teens involve drinking.

Alcohol abuse among teens is also the cause of serious accidents. Thousands of young people aged sixteen to twenty-four are killed each year in alcohol-related incidents of all kinds, according to the National Council on Alcoholism. These include drownings, suicides, violent incidents, homicides, and injuries from fire.

An anti-drunk driving message appears beside a liquor advertisement on a billboard in Harrisburg, Pennsylvania. What is the effect of these conflicting messages on youths in our society?

Drinking and driving

One of society's greatest problems is drunken driving. Almost half of the forty-five thousand drivers

killed in traffic accidents have a high blood alcohol content.

The chances of having an accident increase seven times when a driver has a blood alcohol level of 0.10. But even one drink can affect a person's ability to drive well. And the chances of having an accident double from just two drinks.

Traffic accidents involving alcohol are the leading cause of death for people aged sixteen to twenty-four. About 10,000 are killed and another 220,000 young people are injured. And driving while drinking is not uncommon. One-fourth of high school students report they have driven while intoxicated at least three times. One in three admit they have ridden in cars with a drunk driver.

In most states, driving with a BAC of 0.10 or more is against the law. Police can stop drivers suspected of being drunk. Suspects are given a test that shows their blood alcohol level. If it is above the legal limit, the police or highway patrol officer can

A beer can is embedded in the dashboard of a car involved in a head-on collision that killed four people. Alcohol-related traffic accidents are a leading cause of death among young people.

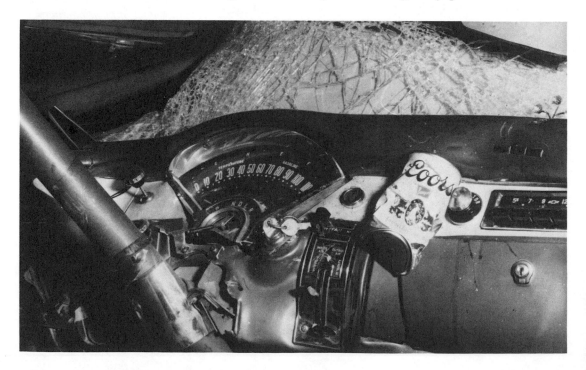

arrest them for driving while intoxicated (DWI).

Persons who drive while intoxicated can lose their licenses, be fined, and be sent to a school where they learn about the social problems caused by drinking and driving. If a person has many DWI arrests, a judge could send him or her to jail.

The penalties are more severe when the drunk driver is involved in an accident. A drunk driver who kills someone can be arrested for murder.

Kevin Tunell of Virginia was a senior in high school when he left a party after drinking. His car hit an oncoming vehicle and killed a teenage girl. He was charged and found guilty of driving while intoxicated. His sentence required that he tell his story to groups of high school students.

Kevin describes himself as a typical teenager who got good grades and was looking forward to college. Although friends had offered to drive him home the night of the accident, Kevin assured them that he was all right and could handle it.

The days after the accident were particularly difficult for Kevin. Every newscast reported the crash. People wrote letters to the newspaper, demanding that he be sent to jail for what he had done. At his trial, the parents of the girl he had killed told the judge they wanted to see Kevin spend time in jail. Even though he had the support of his family, at times Kevin got so depressed that he felt "the walls were going to close in on me."

In Moscow, a poster warns of the dangers of drinking and street crime. The caption reads: "Everywhere, any time, in any situation, let us combat drunks and hooligans."

Drunken-driving laws

Many countries have stricter drinking-and-driving legislation than the United States. For example, drunken drivers in Finland, Sweden, England, and France receive automatic jail sentences and lose their licenses for at least a year. In El Salvador and Bulgaria, they are executed. These countries have fewer problems with drinking and driving.

States have tried to reduce the number of acci-

In France, a woman takes a sobriety test in a police van following legalization of random testing in 1978. Alcohol abuse is a problem affecting countries across the globe.

dents involving young people and alcohol by raising the minimum drinking age. These laws make it illegal for teens under a certain age to purchase alcohol. They also make it illegal to sell alcohol to persons under the minimum age.

In most states this age is twenty-one. In the early 1970s, however, twenty-four states lowered the minimum age to eighteen. Their reasoning was that eighteen-year-olds were old enough to vote and to serve in the armed forces. Therefore, why should they not also be allowed to purchase alcohol?

However, accidents and deaths involving alcohol increased after the ages were lowered. By contrast, various studies showed that accident fatalities decreased by 28 percent for persons aged eighteen to twenty-one when the minimum drinking age was raised. In 1984, Congress passed a bill that encouraged states to change their laws. The law reduced federal funds for building highways to states that did not raise their drinking age to twenty-one. Most states raised the age.

Despite the grave problems alcoholism causes, many teenagers have successfully stopped a heavy drinking habit. Mark J. was finally able to see that his life was out of control. With treatment and a desire to become sober, Mark finally changed his life-style and gave up drinking.

"Life is definitely changing for the better," he said.

4

Treatment of
Alcoholism

THERE ARE ABOUT thirty-three hundred treatment centers for alcoholism in the United States. Of the more than 450,000 people who receive treatment, 22 percent are twenty years old or younger. The cost of treatment for alcoholism in the United States each year is $13 billion.

Despite all of these efforts, no one has developed a sure remedy for alcoholism. But understanding of the problem and treatment of it have improved.

History of treatment

Until recently, most treatment programs focused on punishing the alcoholic. In ancient Egypt, laws called for flogging or jailing drunkards. In the sixth century A.D., monks who were too drunk to sing during mass were sent to bed without supper.

Persons caught drunk in early America or England during the 1700s were fined. If they could not pay the fine, they were locked into stocks (wooden devices used to hold people in place, usually for public display) or they were forced to wear a large wooden barrel with a hole at the top for their heads. This was supposed to embarrass them into not drinking.

(opposite page) In the nineteenth century, alcoholics were treated as criminals, as this lithograph illustrates.

65

The ancient Greeks in Sparta had an unusual way of encouraging their children to avoid alcohol: they made their slaves get drunk in front of the children. They thought that this would show the children how foolish drunkards were.

Many societies developed myths about preventing drunkenness. The Chinese believed that if a person held a precious stone under the tongue when drinking, the person would not get drunk. The Egyptians thought eating boiled cabbage leaves while drinking would ward off drunkenness. The Romans ate bitter almonds for protection. Of course, none of these "cures" did any good. Society has also tried to control drunkenness by controlling the taverns. English law required tavern owners to buy licenses to serve alcohol as early as the 1400s. Lawmakers thought this would reduce the number of licenses and thus limit the number of taverns that served alcohol. The law also allowed lawmakers to remove the licenses of tavern owners who allowed drunk and disorderly

Monument of the Syrian soldier Terrura, with his son and wife, sipping beer through a cane.

conduct. English judges regulated the number of taverns in each town. Anyone caught keeping an illegal one could be publicly flogged.

Beginning in the 1700s, Americans saw alcoholism as a moral weakness and temperance was encouraged as the way to avoid alcoholism. But simply telling people not to drink did not work because of the addictive properties of alcohol.

During this time alcoholism was also considered a form of insanity or mental illness. Those alcoholics too sick to care for themselves were placed in mental hospitals.

The idea that alcoholism is a disease and not a moral problem existed as long ago as ancient Greece. But it was not until the late 1800s that treatment of alcoholism became the business of physicians.

The first American hospital for alcoholics was

Drunkenness and disorderly conduct were common occurrences throughout Europe in the sixteenth and seventeenth centuries.

A young alcoholic sits huddled in an early mental hospital. Beginning in the 1700s, alcoholism was considered a form of mental illness.

opened in Boston in 1868. Although it was called Home for the Fallen, it was an attempt at treating alcoholics more sympathetically.

Despite the attempts to see the alcoholic as any other person with an illness, until 1970 the most common treatment of problem drinkers was imprisonment. Drunks were often picked up by police and thrown into jail, where they would go through a painful withdrawal from alcohol without medical help. When they were sober, they were released. Many of them went through this process again and again.

In 1970, however, Congress passed a law that called for more humane treatment of alcoholics. Drunkenness is no longer a crime unless a person is driving. Instead, most persons found drunk in public today are taken to centers known as detoxification or detox centers.

Detoxing, or waiting until the body rids itself of the toxins of alcohol, can take one or several days. Patients may be given medicine that helps them get through withdrawal. They are cared for by personnel who are trained to work with alcoholics. They are also evaluated to identify medical or psychological needs. When they are sober, patients are given information about various treatment centers for alcoholics. If the patient has been in trouble with the law, the court may require him or her to get further treatment to help stop the drinking behavior. Some cities have special detox centers that are just for teenagers. In other places, teen alcoholics go through withdrawal at a treatment center. It is not possible for an

A counselor from a detoxification center in Louisiana talks to a youth about the effects of alcohol on one's health.

A speaker talks to fellow Alcoholics Anonymous members at a meeting. Posters on the wall refer to the program's twelve-step recovery plan.

alcoholic to enter treatment until he or she has gone through withdrawal.

More than 95 percent of today's programs for alcoholics use the same twenty-eight day treatment plan. Called the Hazelden Model, it was developed in Minnesota in the early 1950s. The plan was built on many of the principles of a self-help group started in 1935 called Alcoholics Anonymous.

Alcoholics Anonymous

Bill Wilson, the founder of Alcoholics Anonymous, was an American stockbroker during the 1920s. His drinking problem was causing him problems with his marriage, work, and health. Often Bill's wife would find him passed out in their apartment entrance. He was in and out of hospitals.

Although Bill W. had tried many times to stop drinking, he was not able to do so. He had looked for answers everywhere, and read and done research on his problem. Finally he wondered if God could help him. He was not a religious man, but one night he asked God for help.

As Bill described it, the room lit up with a great white light. Bill felt an ecstasy that he found hard to describe. He felt as if he was in another world. All around him he sensed the presence of peace.

After that spiritual experience, Bill W. was able to stop drinking. He shared his experience with a physician who was also an alcoholic. Together the two men formed a self-help group to give themselves and others support to stay away from alcohol. Group meetings stressed the need for alcoholics to trust a "power greater than themselves" in order to "recover."

Alcoholics Anonymous (AA) groups grew steadily, and soon they had spread around the world. These meetings are still very popular today. Many thousands of alcoholics have received help from them. AA groups still follow the "Twelve Steps to Recovery" that Bill W. outlined in a book he published about AA called *The Big Book*. Some meetings are especially for teenage alcoholics.

Alcoholics Anonymous has no membership requirements or dues. A person may go to AA meetings on his or her own without being in a treatment program. Other AA meetings are held at treatment centers as a part of the program. Clients often are encouraged to attend AA meetings on their own after they finish treatment.

Treatment centers for teens

Teenage alcoholics are treated in separate programs from adults. Unlike adults, teens have usually been alcoholic for only a year or two. Teenagers also have special needs such as finishing school, choosing a career, and learning dating skills. Like those for adults, most treatment programs for teens follow the Hazelden Model. But they also take into account each teen's unique situation.

Bill Wilson founded Alcoholics Anonymous to provide support to alcoholics across the country.

Teens are treated for alcoholism in either outpatient or inpatient settings. Those in inpatient care move to a treatment center and live there, usually for six weeks. Teens in outpatient care may still live at home and come to the center each day for treatment. Treatment programs vary, but a typical program will have the following parts.

First, teens receive support—that is, approval and encouragement—for staying off alcohol. They are given opportunities to replace alcohol with such things as athletics, success with schoolwork, and friendships.

The programs also offer structure. Students are expected to take classes and/or to work at a job. They attend various lectures, therapy sessions, and group meetings, including Alcoholics Anonymous. If they follow the rules, they are given privileges. If not, they lose privileges.

Counselors help teen alcoholics get to know themselves better and develop better social skills. They help them learn ways to control their behavior. Counselors stress the positive, telling the teens over and over again in many ways that they can succeed.

Because the counselors are friendly and support-ive, the teens usually come to view them as friends. Soon the teens find themselves sharing their unique problems with a counselor.

Then together the counselor and the teenager make a plan to help the teen overcome his or her ad-diction. The plan is very specific. It states exactly

Pivot House in Connecticut operates on a "cold turkey" approach to alcoholism. Here, a young resident talks about addiction and recovery.

A family sits amid empty drink cans and other rubble in Glasgow, Scotland, where alcoholism is becoming a major social problem.

what the teen must do to complete the plan. This might include getting a high school diploma and/or job skills, or making a new set of friends. As the teen works through the plan, the counselor is there to offer support.

Often a program uses peer pressure. For example, if one person leaves a can of soda in the lounge, all may lose soda privileges. So another teenager will confront the teen, pointing out that he or she is breaking the rules. In this way, the teens get an accurate view of their own behavior. Those who have been in the program for a while can help those who are new.

Because alcoholism is often a family problem, many programs include family therapy. A teenager's family may come to the center once a week. Together they meet with a therapist who helps them solve problems and plan for the future.

Treatment also takes into consideration a teen's high energy level. Time is planned for recreation such as swimming or playing volleyball. This also gives teens healthy ways to work on friendships and social skills.

Recovery, or staying off alcohol after treatment

Some teens live in halfway houses after they finish treatment for alcoholism. Others may go home to live. Before they leave, many sign a no-use contract, promising they will not use alcohol. Teens are encouraged to attend AA meetings for teenagers, and to develop new friends who do not use alcohol.

Society has come a long way in its treatment of alcoholics. Still, the success rate is not very high. The number of alcoholics who stay off alcohol for three years after treatment is only about 25 percent.

The ones who make it are those teens who refuse to drink even socially and who continue to attend AA, according to Jim Heaslip. Once a teenage alcoholic himself, he has attended AA meetings for over thirty years.

Heaslip compares being an alcoholic to having an allergy to strawberries. "If you break out today from eating strawberries, you'll do so ten years from now," he says. The same is true for alcoholics, he adds; if they are addicted to it today, they will be so ten years from now. So, continued support for staying sober is necessary, sometimes for a lifetime.

Going through a program for alcoholism is only 5 percent of treatment, Heaslip claims. Aftercare, or avoiding alcohol in the future, is the other 95 percent.

Even with the help of AA, relapses are common. Teen alcoholics are encouraged to accept their setbacks but to continue attending AA and avoiding alcohol in the future. Those who attend AA meetings regularly call this "working the program."

Those who work with alcoholics are always looking for new ways to treat the disease. At least one counselor has developed a treatment program that includes what she calls biochemical repair.

Biochemical repair

In 1975, Joan Mathews-Larson's son had just finished treatment for teen alcoholism. He was struggling to remain sober at a halfway house. One minute he would be fine, she recalls, and the next minute he was in a rage. He could not seem to control his emotions.

Finally, one evening Mathews-Larson's son lost the battle with alcoholism and committed suicide. His mother was devastated. She was determined to find out why her son died.

Now Joan Mathews-Larson runs a center for alcoholics called Health Recovery Center. She discovered that alcoholics have chemically altered brains. Besides the treatment offered by the Hazelden Model, alcoholics need help to restore their bodies to health. Many of the symptoms of addiction, such as fatigue, irritability, depression, and tremors, continue even after the alcoholic is sober. Without the needed biochemical repair, they may not be physically able to overcome their craving for alcohol, says Mathews-Larson.

Many times she finds that her clients have other physical addictions besides alcohol. All are tested for hypoglycemia (decrease in blood sugar), food and chemical allergies, and chronic yeast problems or infections. Their thyroid function is checked. Then they are given vitamins, minerals, and special diets to help restore their health.

With treatment for these physical problems, an alcoholic can get rid of cravings, Mathews-Larson says. Depression and mood swings often clear up as well. But the client may have to change many habits. Most clients must give up sugar and junk food. They learn to eat healthy foods and take care of their bodies. Regular exercise is also an important part of the program.

Joan Mathews-Larson's clients show a 75 percent rate of recovery, she says. Her work in the field of biochemical repair may be an important part of alcohol treatment in the future.

5

The Alcohol Industry

ONE REASON THAT alcohol has become so important to society is that it is big business in the United States. For example, in 1986 the alcohol industry produced and sold about 186 million barrels of beer at a profit of almost $1 billion. (A barrel contains about 31 gallons.) That is almost 24 gallons of beer per person! The alcohol industry also produced and sold 2.5 gallons of wine and 1.6 gallons of distilled spirits per person in 1986. Together the alcohol industry contributes about $52 billion to the U.S. economy each year and employs over 3.2 million people.

Because the alcohol industry has been a profitable one for a long time in the United States, it is firmly ingrained in American society. Consumers buy its products. In turn, effective promotion, including easy availability and widespread advertising by the industry, creates increased interest in buying alcoholic beverages.

(opposite page) In 1986, California Coolers kicked off a winter advertising campaign with this picture. This promotion was designed to convince young people that wine coolers are a year-round drink.

The industry's roots in American history

The alcohol industry has been active in America since the time of the early colonies. Among the first settlers were brewers who turned much of the colonies' barley crops into beer. Because the brewers bought the farmers' barley, this arrangement was profitable for both groups.

The first distillery for the making of hard liquor was built in 1640 by Dutch settlers on Staten Island in what is now New York. At first the Dutch made brandywine and gin from local berries and barley. But when the English took over the Dutch colony in 1664, they used the distillery to make rum from molasses imported from England.

Another distilled spirit made in early America was whiskey. The distillation of whiskey provided a larger market for corn and rye. Farmers in Kentucky found it profitable to turn their crops into whiskey before transporting them across the mountains to New England. That was because whiskey, a concentrated form of corn or rye, took less space and therefore less money to transport than the raw grains. It

Workers monitor a distillery in one of many such American establishments.

Guests tour the Jack Daniels distillery in Lynchburg, Tennessee. The economy of the county depends on the distillery for its livelihood.

could also be stored more easily and did not spoil. Whiskey became even more popular and therefore more profitable in America during the revolutionary war when it was difficult to get molasses from overseas to make rum.

German immigrants in the 1800s were responsible for starting many of the large beer breweries in cities such as New York, Milwaukee, and St. Louis. Frederic Miller, for example, brought the brewing craft with him from Germany when he immigrated in 1855. He bought a tiny brewery in Milwaukee that produced only three hundred barrels in its first year of operation.

In 1988 the Miller Brewing Company produced more than forty million barrels of beer a year at seven location across the United States. Its brands include Miller High Life, Miller Genuine Draft, Miller Lite, Lowenbrau, Meister Brau, and Milwaukee's Best. It also operated five can-manufacturing plants, one bottle-manufacturing plant, a carton-manufacturing plant, and six distributorships that deliver beer to retailers. These businesses employed more than ten thousand workers. The total profits for 1988 were $190 million, up from $114 million in 1984.

A liquor store manager stands amidst rows of beer, wine, and various liquors. The alcohol industry has been a profitable one in the United States.

Because of its size, the alcohol industry plays a strong role in U.S. economics. *Economics* is a science that deals with the making and selling of products. Because there are so many products made and sold in the United States, it is a very complex science. The buying and selling of one product affects other products and services.

For example, if customers buy less whiskey one year, many people are affected. The store or tavern that sells whiskey makes a smaller profit. The distiller who makes the whiskey ends up with a surplus and also loses money. Executives at the distillery may believe they will sell less whiskey the following year, too, so they distill less in order to save money, causing layoffs of employees.

In turn, the distiller buys less corn or rye from the farmer. Now the farmer has lost money and therefore does not invest in a new tractor or other farm equipment. This hurts the local farm-equipment dealer. The farmer also cannot afford to buy as many other products such as shoes, television sets, and microwave ovens. So other store owners lose profits, too.

On the other hand, increased sales of alcoholic beverages bring more profit not only to the manufacturers, but also to store and tavern owners, distributors, and farmers. Together their success makes the U.S. economy a strong one.

Taxes and the alcohol industry

Government involvement in the form of taxes can affect the sale of alcoholic beverages, too. A tax on alcohol makes it more expensive. Economists tell us that when the price of a product goes up, fewer people will buy it; when the price goes down, more people will buy it.

Alcoholic beverages have always been heavily taxed. Excise taxes, paid by the manufacturer, on beer, wine, and distilled spirits in 1982 came to $5.8 billion for local and state governments, and $5.7 billion for the federal government. State and local sales taxes, paid by the consumer, amounted to another $2.1 billion in 1982. When other taxes such as income, property, and inventory taxes are added, the

An Anheuser Busch beer ad. Like other businesses, alcohol manufacturers spend a great deal of time planning effective advertising strategies.

A 150-case lot of wine ages at a vineyard in Litchfield, Connecticut. Sophisticated brewing and distilling equipment has enabled manufacturers to meet consumers' increasing demand for alcohol.

alcohol industry pays more than $20 billion a year in taxes.

Some lawmakers have proposed raising the federal excise tax on alcohol in hopes that it will cut consumption. This tactic to reduce the problems caused by heavy drinking has been supported by a study done by Philip Cook of the Institute for Public Policy Studies at Duke University. His study showed that a 30 percent increase in the retail price of alcoholic beverages could curtail the amount consumed by a similar 30 percent.

In addition, a few states are considering adding their own taxes to alcoholic beverages as a way to pay for the expensive law enforcement of DWI offenses. A law being considered in Minnesota would add a nickel tax per drink—about 30 cents to the price of a six-pack of beer; 40 cents to a quart of wine; $1.10 to a fifth of 86 proof liquor.

But legislators are concerned that many heavy drinkers would simply drive to a nearby state and stock up on alcohol. This would hurt local liquor sales but not necessarily cut consumption. And a law that encourages people to drive to another state to purchase alcohol could put more drunk drivers on the road.

The alcohol industry, of course, wants low taxes on alcoholic beverages because high taxes cause less of their product to be sold. Together, not only the manufacturers but also the distributors, the tavern and store owners, and the farmers send powerful lobbyists to Washington. These lobbyists encourage members of Congress to vote against bills that raise taxes on alcoholic beverages.

Promotion

Despite paying large amounts of money in taxes, the alcohol industry makes a profit. Like other businesses, it remains successful by increasing sales of alcoholic beverages through promotion.

One way companies promote their products is by making them more available to consumers. The alcohol industry has worked hard to make alcoholic beverages more available over recent years. Bars and liquor stores have stayed open for more hours. More liquor stores have opened at neighborhood shopping centers. The increased availability has increased profits for the alcohol industry.

Another way that manufacturers promote their products is through widespread and effective advertising. Large businesses in America spend a great deal of time and money planning their marketing strategies. First, they do studies that give them statistics on who uses their products. This helps them plan their ads to reach those consumers. These businesses also survey those who do not use a product to find out why. Then they try to find a way to interest that group in buying the product, such as offering free samples or telling about its benefits in a TV commercial.

A company's ads are specially designed by experts to appeal to the goals, desires, and fantasies of a target audience using the data collected. The advertisers want people to think, "If I use that product, I'll be like the people I see in the ads." For example, a wine ad showing a group of wealthy people enjoying a cruise on a yacht indirectly leads viewers to assume that drinking this brand of wine will make them happy and wealthy, too.

Many companies use famous spokespersons to sell their products. For example, a commercial for Meister Brau beer features actor George Wendt from NBC's "Cheers." The image of Wendt as a regular bar customer on the show can only serve to enhance Meister Brau as the preferred beer at the bar in "Cheers" in the minds of viewers.

Together, U.S. brewers, vintners (wine makers), and distillers spend over $1 billion each year to advertise their products. About 60 percent of the money spent (about $800 million) goes toward beer

An advertisement from the U.S. Department of Transportation is designed to counteract alcohol ads that promote excessive drinking.

U.S. Department of Transportation

DRINKING AND DRIVING CAN KILL A FRIENDSHIP.

advertisements. Wine and distilled spirits each account for about 20 percent of the remainder of the advertising market for alcohol.

Ethical concerns in advertising

The alcohol industry faces a unique dilemma in marketing its products because of the problems of overdrinking. Critics have asked whether or not it is ethical for a company to convince people to buy their product if the product causes health and social problems. The alcohol industry has in turn been faced with the problem of promoting a product in a way that does not encourage drinking to excess.

The alcohol industry claims that its ads are aimed at people who already drink, and are trying only to convince drinkers to switch to the advertiser's brand. An expert often quoted by the alcohol industry is researcher C. B. Popescu who in 1983 concluded that ". . . advertising does not significantly increase overall consumption of alcoholic beverages. . . ." His studies, however, do nothing to prove that advertising does not promote abuse of alcohol.

The Center for Science in the Public Interest recently published a book called *The Booze Merchants*. The book is very critical of advertising by the alcohol industry. In it, authors Michael Jacobson, Robert Atkins, and George Hacker give many facts and statistics about alcohol advertising. After examining ads, they conclude that alcohol ads in general *do* try to persuade nonconsumers to purchase alcohol. The authors argue that it would be unreasonable for the advertisers not to pursue new drinkers. The underlying principle of any business, in order to stay in business, must be to expand its market.

The authors also claim that many alcohol ads encourage alcohol abuse, especially among working men and sports fans. Heavy drinkers, including alcoholics, consume 50-70 percent of all alcoholic beverages sold in the United States. As the authors of *The Booze Merchants* point out, when a heavy drinker starts to drink less or stops drinking altogether, the industry loses sales.

Does advertising increase alcohol use?

The book contains the findings of studies on the advertising of alcoholic beverages. One recent study by two University of Michigan researchers, for example, concluded that advertising increases alcohol use and prompts people, especially teenagers, to overuse alcohol.

The Booze Merchants concedes that a few ads appear to promote drinking in moderation. Seagrams Distiller Company, for example, uses the phrase, "enjoy our quality in moderation." Its Crown Royal ad states, "We tip our hat to all the fathers of the world who've taught their children the values of drinking only in moderation."

Many companies even provide materials for education and the prevention of alcohol abuse. For example, the Miller Brewing Company provides educational materials to distributors, bars, and restaurants on how to promote responsible drinking.

Should alcohol ads be regulated?

Various organizations within the alcohol industry have tried to self-regulate advertising by adopting codes of ethics that set standards for ads. These groups are: the United States Brewers Association, the Wine Institute, and the Distilled Spirits Council of the United States. The codes prohibit advertising hard liquors on television and radio, for example. They also discourage ads that show actual drinking or any signs of drunkenness. Other taboos are linking alcohol to crime, using obscene material, or showing young people drinking. Companies are not required to follow the codes of ethics, but some do so voluntarily.

Critics think alcohol advertising should be regu-

A young man is tested for signs of intoxication. Some studies conclude that advertising increases alcohol abuse among young people.

lated and restricted by the government. The authors of *The Booze Merchants* point to the many ads that break the alcohol industry's advertising codes. For example, a recent Budweiser ad showed lumberjacks using giant chain saws. This ad violates the code of ethics for beer brewers, which states that "Beer advertisements should not link beer drinking with activities and situations which require a high degree of alertness."

Perhaps alcohol advertising could be regulated in the same way that ads for tobacco products are regulated. When the U.S. Surgeon General found that tobacco caused health problems, tobacco advertising was restricted. Tobacco ads are not allowed on either radio or television because these media are licensed by the government to serve the public interest. Ads for cigarettes are permitted elsewhere, such as in magazines and on billboards, but they must contain a health warning.

So far, not many restrictions on alcohol advertising exist. The Federal Trade Commission regulates advertising, and it forbids "unfair or deceptive" advertising. But it says nothing specific about alcohol. In the meantime, the attacks by critics and replies by the alcohol industry continue in full force.

Ads that target young people

Many ads for alcoholic beverages are designed to appeal to young people. For example, a recent ad for Pabst Blue Ribbon showed a class of students dozing during a lecture. The caption read, "After a real fascinating lecture, study the *real* taste of beer." Such ads are common, even though the U.S. Brewers Association code states, "Brewers should not aim their advertising at the young."

Those who work with teenage alcohol abuse are concerned about such ads. They say that teens are vulnerable and not always able to tell the difference between the settings for ads and real-life situations.

Almost half of the ads in magazines that appeal to young people, such as *Rolling Stone* and *National Lampoon,* are for alcoholic beverages. Ads for alcohol are common in college newspapers, even though many college students are younger than the minimum drinking age of twenty-one set in most states.

A recent ad in *Newsweek On Campus* read, "Lite beer is like quarterbacks. We can't wait to knock 'em down." Another ad for Rumple Minze peppermint schnapps was found in Michigan State University's student newspaper. It shows a young man asking a friend why he is not "scoring" with women. His friend asks, "Do you have Rumple Minze in your freezer?" The ad implies that college men should have this product so they can attract women.

Various companies even admit that they target young people with ads for alcohol. A spokesperson for PepsiCo Wine and Spirits stated its goal as "to get the attention of the entry-level consumer." Another marketing executive said, "Let's not forget that getting a [college] freshman to choose a certain brand of beer may mean that he will maintain his brand loyalty for the next 20 to 35 years."

Adolph Coors Company pitches its Herman Joseph's beer to men ages eighteen to twenty-four. This brand of beer contains 10 percent more alcohol than regular Coors beer. The authors of *The Booze Merchants* accuse Coors of marketing this high-alcohol-content beer to young men in an attempt to hook them on alcohol.

Events sponsored by alcoholic beverage companies

Some colleges even have representatives of beer companies who work on their campuses. These people promote their products by sponsoring parties for organizations such as fraternities. They give away free beer and door prizes in exchange for an opportunity to introduce college students to their prod-

The alcohol industry targets this age group with promotions for alcohol at rock concerts, sporting events, and contests.

ucts. One ad in the University of Hawaii paper said, "Having a Party? See Chuck Parker, Your Budweiser Campus Representative." A phone number was also listed.

Miller Brewing Company has sponsored contests in which students can win prizes such as television sets or pool tables for saving empty beer cans. Pabst ran a sweepstakes in which students could win up to thirteen thousand dollars in tuition fees. Such promotions, according to *The Booze Merchants,* encourage young people to drink.

Many alcoholic beverage companies sponsor rock concerts as a way to promote their products, to reach young people through the kind of entertainment they enjoy. The sponsorship includes giveaways of T-shirts and posters that feature the logo of a brand of alcohol. This promotion is aimed at underage consumers, as the average age of rock concertgoers is fifteen to eighteen.

Also, young people are exposed to drinking by watching television. Many children learn through watching TV that drinking is a normal part of life. According to the National Institute of Mental Health, the average child sees ten television shows that involve drinking each day. That is three thousand examples a year!

In addition, these young viewers are exposed to beer ads meant for an older audience. According to a 1987 study, American children between the ages of two and eighteen view around 100,00 beer commercials each year.

Whether or not the marketing and sale of alcohol add to it, the problem of teen alcoholism is a complex issue. Even the experts do not agree. But it is not surprising that many teenagers have conflicting and confusing attitudes about drinking alcohol, given the widespread influence of the alcohol industry in the United States.

I wanted to be like my dad, "Order me a dry martini."

It's not easy to say no when your friends, your parents and everyone around you is drinking.

But alcohol is a drug. And you can get hooked on it.

It's a fact. The younger you start, the more addictive it is and the more damage it can do.

It's not easy to say no. But if you want to be somebody, you have to learn.

To find out more, contact the National Council on Alcoholism in your area. Or write NCA, 12 West 21st Street, New York, N.Y. 10010.

Say no.
And say yes to your life.

National Council on Alcoholism Inc.

6

Prevention and Education

THERE IS NO EASY WAY to prevent teen alcoholism. Laws that make it illegal to drive while intoxicated and that raise the minimum drinking age have helped alleviate the problem. The government has also tried heavy taxation as a means of making alcoholic beverages more expensive and less available to teenagers. But many parts of a community, including parents, schools, and teens themselves, must work together to solve the problem of teen alcoholism.

What parents can do

A survey of community leaders and those who work in the field of chemical dependency showed that they expect parents to take a dominant role in the prevention of teen alcoholism. Yet many parents feel inadequately equipped to raise alcohol-free children.

In their book on teen alcoholism, Carmella and John Bartimole give parents tips on raising children to drink responsibly. According to them, developing good communication skills with children by listening, respecting, and understanding them is a good start. Parents can also tell their children that it is

(opposite page) A National Council on Alcoholism advertisement encourages young people to say no to alcohol.

okay to talk to them and ask questions about alcohol.

Parents can educate their children about the dangers of alcohol, the problems of drinking and driving, and the DWI laws. According to the Bartimoles, talking directly to young people about alcohol and its effects is the best way.

Children need firm rules and guidelines regarding alcohol, according to the Bartimoles. Rules should be specific: is it ever okay to drink, and if so, when? The consequences of breaking the rules must also be spelled out and carried out.

Parents also can help their children avoid problems with alcohol by encouraging high self-esteem, as statistics show that children who abuse alcohol have low self-esteem. Parents who say such things

Artist John Carlton of the Associated Press presented this drawing to illustrate the severity of the nation's problem with alcoholism.

as "How stupid can you be?" and "You never do anything right" are harming their children's self-esteem. According to the Bartimoles, parents can help their children develop good self-esteem by praising them, accepting them, and avoiding negative labels and put-downs.

The best education parents can provide is to set a good example, according to the Bartimoles. Children who see their parents treating alcohol responsibly are likely to treat it responsibly as well.

What schools can do

Most schools offer drug-education programs. These programs are designed for students who do not yet have a problem with alcohol or drugs. Their purpose is to give students the tools necessary to make responsible decisions regarding the use of alcohol and other drugs.

The alcohol and drug-education programs that are the most effective stress exploring one's own attitudes toward alcohol and developing communication skills, self-esteem, and the skills for making decisions about using alcohol. Other units in a class on drug prevention might include facts about alcohol, the possible effects of alcohol abuse in the family, and the individual rights and responsibilities toward the use of alcohol.

One highly praised program called Here's Looking At You, Too was developed in Seattle, Washington. It stresses the need to provide classes in alcohol prevention starting in kindergarten. Students from kindergarten on can be taught that it is okay to ask questions about alcohol. Often they have received the message that drinking is bad, but then are confused when they see their favorite TV heroes or their parents drink alcohol. Asking questions can help them sort out these conflicting messages.

Another excellent program called CASPAR (Cambridge and Somerville Program for Alcohol

Rehabilitation) was developed in Massachusetts. It encourages students to share openly and honestly about their own attitudes toward alcohol. It also stresses opportunities for students to role-play in real-life situations. A teacher or group leader, for example, may give the class a setting, perhaps a party in which they are offered a drink. Then students act out the situation as a skit, getting first-hand experience in saying no to someone who offers them a beer.

Studies have shown that children in the fourth through sixth grades are at a good age to learn about alcohol-abuse prevention. They are old enough to understand the issues, but most have not yet been faced with the decision of whether or not to drink alcohol, especially among friends. It is important that they be given information and tools for making

This cartoon, published by Coors, appears on a poster that is distributed throughout high schools and universities.

THE PARTY ENDS HERE

decisions *before* they need it.

Teachers need up-to-date information to be adequately prepared to teach drug education. Effective teachers understand their students' attitudes about drinking, as attitudes toward alcohol differ from community to community. They also have a strong interest in the subject and are committed to helping students sort out society's conflicting messages regarding the use of alcohol.

Teachers in turn need access to good materials and time to study and prepare for class. They also need the support of counselors, principals, parents, and the community in general.

Regardless of what law enforcement, parents, or schools do, it is really up to the individual child or teenager to decide whether or not to abuse alcohol. No one else can make that decision for him or her.

Nancy Reagan joins students at a Just Say No assembly at an elementary school. She started this campaign to keep young people off alcohol and other drugs.

The best thing students can do is equip themselves with information about alcohol. Knowing the facts will help them make good decisions.

Many teens who come from alcoholic homes have been able to avoid having drinking problems themselves by attending meetings for children of alcoholics. Here they have a chance to discuss family problems with other children their own age and to receive support for staying away from alcohol and other drugs.

Other children join groups such as Just Say No clubs where they promise not to drink. The Just Say No campaign was started by Nancy Reagan, the wife of President Ronald Reagan, as a way to keep

Football player Eric Dickerson in action. Dickerson devotes off-field time to talking with young people about the hazards of drugs and alcohol.

kids off drugs and alcohol.

She also encouraged people such as Eric Dickerson, the famous football player who holds the record for running more yards in one season than any other running back in the National Football League, to sponsor clubs for children. Children who joined Eric's "team" were called Dickerson Rangers. They met with him to hear him talk about alcohol and drugs. Those who promised to say no to drugs received free Ranger T-shirts and were often bused to football games to watch Eric Dickerson play.

Some schools have active student groups to help teens avoid drinking and driving. One group, Students Against Driving Drunk (SADD), was started by a teacher who had lost two of his students to drunken-driving accidents. Students who belong to SADD sign a contract promising not to drink and drive. They also wear buttons and stickers that encourage other students not to drink and drive.

SADD members may receive permission from their school principals to put up posters warning against drinking and driving before a holiday or an event where students often drink. Their motto is "If we dream it, it can be done." Over sixteen thousand chapters of SADD currently operate in junior high and middle schools, high schools, and colleges across the country.

With the help of these groups and other alcohol- and drug-education programs, teenagers are becoming more aware of the components of a healthy lifestyle. As they learn about healthy living, more are choosing better, safer alternatives to alcohol.

Developing a healthy lifestyle

Allan Luks and Joseph Barbato wrote a book about alcohol called *You Are What You Drink*. Both were social drinkers, but after learning about the risks of drinking alcohol, they were determined to find safer ways to feel good and to share their findings with others. They call their way the Twenty-Minute High. Many teens have found their suggestions helpful.

To get the Twenty-Minute High, Luks and Barbato suggest that persons exercise or relax for twenty minutes each day. This, they say in their book, produces highs not unlike the high people get from drinking. "The more you practice, the more intense will be your satisfaction," they claim.

Scientists now think that exercise stimulates the release of endorphins in the brain. Endorphins are chemicals made by the brain that create a natural high.

Practicing relaxation also brings about physical changes. A recent study shows that relaxation reduces stress by releasing a brain chemical that helps people react to stressful situations.

Gradually, society's attitudes toward alcohol are changing. Community leaders are becoming more aware of the complex issues that contribute to teen alcoholism, such as peer pressure and family patterns. Teenagers in turn are becoming better educated about themselves and the risks of alcohol. As the community, school, parents, and teenagers work together, many of the problems of teen alcoholism can be solved.

Appendix

Are You an Alcoholic?

HOW MANY drinking teenagers presently are hooked, or partly hooked, on alcohol cannot be known. For any young person who drinks—who, in fact, may be secretly troubled by his or her drinking—the Youth Information Branch of the Alcoholism Council of Greater Los Angeles has come up with a questionnaire that can prove helpful.

The questions are patterned after the twenty questions used by Johns Hopkins University Hospital to decide whether or not a patient is a problem drinker or alcoholic.

As with the Johns Hopkins questions, it is suggested that if a young person answers Yes to even one question, it is a warning that he or she may be on the way to becoming an alcoholic. Yes to any two questions and the chances are that alcoholism is a distinct possibility. Three Yes answers mean definite alcoholism.

1. Do you lose time from school due to drinking?

2. Do you drink because you are shy with other people?

3. Do you drink to build up your self-confidence?

4. Do you drink alone?

5. Is drinking affecting your reputation—do you care?

6. Do you drink to escape from study or home worries?

7. Do you feel guilty or bummed after drinking?

8. Does it bother you if somebody says that maybe you drink too much?

9. Do you have to take a drink when you go out on a date?

10. Do you make out generally better when you have a drink?

11. Do you get into financial troubles over buying alcohol?

12. Do you feel a sense of power when you drink?

13. Have you lost friends since you've started drinking?

14. Have you started hanging out with a crowd where alcohol is easy to get?

15. Do your friends drink less than you do?

16. Do you drink until the bottle is done?

17. Have you ever had a complete loss of memory from drinking?

18. Have you ever been to a hospital or been arrested due to drinking and driving?

19. Do you turn off to any studies or lectures about drinking?

20. Do you think you have a problem with alcohol?

National Council on Alcoholism and Drug Dependency, Los Angeles County, Inc.

Glossary

acute alcoholic poisoning: a physical condition caused by excessive drinking of alcohol in which a person's blood alcohol concentration (BAC) reaches 0.40 percent. At this BAC, the person becomes comatose and can die.

alcohol: the intoxicating part of beer, wine, and liquors that is formed during the process of fermentation.

alcoholic beverage or alcoholic drink: a drink that contains alcohol.

Alcoholics Anonymous: a self-help program for alcoholics that includes attending meetings and following the "Twelve Steps to Recovery."

alcoholism: a chronic condition caused by uncontrollable and habitual excessive drinking of alcohol in which a person has become addicted to and physically dependent on alcohol.

beer: an intoxicating drink brewed by allowing grains and yeast to ferment.

biochemical repair: a treatment program for alcoholism that includes physical restoration through the use of food supplements and special diets.

blood alcohol concentration (BAC): the percentage of alcohol in the bloodstream.

bourbon: a liquor made by distilling fermented corn.

brandy: a liquor made by distilling wine or fermented fruit juice.

cirrhosis of the liver: a disease in which liver tissue overworked by processing excessive alcohol becomes scarred and damaged and can no longer process the nutrients in food. It is often fatal.

delerium tremens: a serious form of withdrawal from alcohol characterized by a heightened state of agitation, hallucinations, and intense confusion.

detoxification: the removal of toxins from the body.

distillation: a process during which sugars or grains combine with yeast and water to make alcohol.

fetal alcohol syndrome: a condition in which unborn babies become damaged by the excessive alcohol use by the mother. It can result in damaged organs, birth defects, mental retardation, and/or learning disabilities.

gin: a liquor made by distilling fermented grains and flavored with berries.

hangover: disagreeable physical effects such as headache, nausea, and fatigue following an acute bout of heavy drinking.

Hazelden Model: a treatment program for alcoholism developed in Minnesota, based in part on Alcoholics Anonymous and widely used throughout the world.

heavy drinking: frequent drinking of alcohol to the point of intoxication.

hepatitis: a disease characterized by an inflamed liver, often caused by heavy drinking.

intoxication: an acute impairment caused by a 0.05 percent or more blood alcohol concentration (BAC).

liquor: a distilled alcoholic drink, often sweetened and flavored with fruit.

minimum drinking age: the age at which a person is legally allowed to purchase alcoholic beverages. In most states, the minimum drinking age is twenty-one.

Prohibition: forbidding by law the sale or manufacture of alcoholic beverages.

social drinking: light drinking that does not result in intoxication.

spirits: an intoxicating drink made by distilling beer or wine.

temperance: moderation in or abstinence from alcoholic beverages.

tetrahydroisoquinoline (THIQ): the most addictive substance known to humans, believed to be produced in the brain when alcohol is introduced to those people whose brain chemistry is the type to make the substance.

vodka: a liquor made by distilling fermented barley or other grains.

Wernicke-Korsakoff syndrome: a brain disorder caused by excessive chronic use of alcohol that can lead to severe confusion and dementia, or insanity.

whiskey: a liquor made by distilling fermented barley or rye.

wine: an intoxicating drink made by fermenting grapes.

withdrawal: physical and emotional changes caused when an alcoholic discontinues use of alcohol.

Organizations to Contact

Alcoholics Anonymous World Services, Inc.
P.O. Box 459
Grand Central Station
New York, NY 10163

Alateen and Al-Anon
Al-Anon Family Groups Headquarters
P.O. Box 182
Madison Square Station
New York, NY 10159-0182

Hazelden Educational Materials
P.O. Box 176
Center City, MN 55012-0176
(800) 328-9000

Health Recovery Center, Inc.
3255 Hennepin Avenue South
Minneapolis, MN 55408
(612) 827-7800

National Institute on Alcohol Abuse and Alcoholism
5600 Fishers Lane
Rockville, MD 20857

Remove Intoxicated Drivers (RID)
P.O. Box 520
Schenectady, NY 12301

Students Against Driving Drunk (SADD)
110 Pleasant Street
Corbin Plaza
Marlboro, MA 01752

Suggestions for Further Reading

Claudia Black, *It Will Never Happen to Me*. New York: Random House, 1981.

Chemical Dependency. San Diego: Greenhaven Press, 1984.

Jane Claypool, *Alcohol and You*. New York: Franklin Watts, 1981.

Ross Fishman, Ph.D., *Alcohol and Alcoholism*. New York: Chelsea House, 1986.

Laurel Graeber, *Are You Dying for a Drink?* New York: Julian Messner, 1985.

Edith Lynn Hornik-Beer, *A Teenager's Guide to Living with an Alcoholic Parent*. Center City, MN: Hazelden, 1984.

Margaret O. Hyde, *Alcohol: Uses and Abuses*. Hillside, NJ: Enslow, 1988.

Alan R. Lang, *Alcohol: Teenage Drinking*. New York: Chelsea House, 1985.

Shelly Marshall, *Young, Sober & Free*. Center City, MN: Hazelden, 1978.

Anne Snyder, *My Name Is Davy, I'm an Alcoholic*. New York: New American Library, 1977.

Rob Stephney, *Understanding Drugs: Alcohol*. New York: Franklin Watts, 1987.

Robin S. Wanger, *Sarah T. Portrait of a Teen-Age Alcoholic*. New York: Random House, 1975.

Index

110

About the Author

Nancy J. Nielsen is a communications consultant living in Minneapolis, Minnesota. She specializes in educational materials and has written eight nonfiction books for children.

Ms. Nielsen holds a B.A. Degree in Psychology from St. Olaf College. She has taught school and worked with teenagers living in group homes. She also gives talks and offers writing seminars to groups of students.

When not writing or teaching, Ms. Nielsen can be found whitewater canoeing, or cross-country skiing during the winter months.

Picture Credits